DECADENT
Dinners

DECADENT
Dinners

Marlene van der Westhuizen

BOOK**STORM**   MACMILLAN

ACKNOWLEDGEMENTS

I would love to dedicate this little book to my father and mother, Patens and Petro van Rooyen. Growing up at your table and enjoying noisy dinners whilst looking out over that fabulous Gordon's Bay sea is a huge privilege for all of us … children as well as grandchildren. Thank you.

Also thank you to Basil van Rooyen, Louise Grantham, Lindsey Cohen, René de Wet, Heather Parker, and photographers Stephen Inggs, Gerda Genis and Dawie Verwey. It was, as always, a huge pleasure to work with all of you.

ISBN: 978-1-920434-05-2
First edition, first impression 2010

Published jointly by Bookstorm (Pty) Limited, PO Box 4532, Northcliff, 2115, Johannesburg, South Africa, www.bookstorm.co.za
and Pan Macmillan South Africa, Private Bag X19, Northlands, 2116, Johannesburg, South Africa, www.panmacmillan.co.za

Distributed by Pan Macmillan Via Booksite Afrika

Photography by Stephen Inggs, Gerda Genis and Dawie Verwey
Edited by Content by Design
Proofread by Vanessa Perlman
Design and layout by René de Wet
Printed and bound by Ultra Litho (Pty) Limited

Contents

Preface

The moment we started work on *Lazy Lunches*, we realised that a book on dinners needed to follow really fast on its heels. And here it is! Another little book you can take on holiday with you.

It is redolent of all the places we love to enjoy a meal … under our favourite tree at the bottom of our garden, in front of an old Victorian fireplace or around a yellowwood table with our friends.

This is a happy combination of my favourite 'brasserie luxe' dinner recipes from my previous books, *Delectable* and *Sumptuous*, supplemented by a handful of new dishes we have been loving during the past year at the Food Studio in Green Point, Cape Town.

It is easy, comfortable food that I hope will give you as much pleasure as it does me.

Marlene van der Westhuizen
Cape Town, 2010

Chapter 1

Under the pomegranate tree

On a late autumn afternoon, when the sun draws long and smoky fingers through the pomegranate's branches, I love to throw an old linen tablecloth on the sun-bleached table under the tree. We settle in amongst the falling yellow leaves. The fountain gurgles softly. My husband lights a cigar and pours some champagne. We have a gentle meal, maybe chicken with black olives or lamb with rosemary, while the evening slowly draws to a close.

Pan-fried fillet with mushrooms

Serves 10 generously

*The girl's way of doing a fillet ...
no smelly fires and certainly no ash
over your cashmere.*

- butter
- 25 ml olive oil
- 1 whole fillet
- 1 punnet small mushrooms,
  fried
- 125 ml fresh cream

Heat a large pan and melt a dollop of butter in it. Add the olive oil and wait until it gives off a little smoke. Add the fillet and seal quickly. Turn the heat down a little and let it cook in its own juices, turning regularly, until done. Add the mushrooms and cream. Serve with baby potatoes and lightly caramelised tomatoes.

Potatoes with rosemary

Rosemary goes equally well with potatoes and red meat – serve with the fillet.

- 24 small white potatoes
- 20 sprigs rosemary
- 100 ml olive oil
- salt and pepper

Preheat the oven to 180 deg C/Gas 4. Boil the potatoes in their skins until they are almost cooked through. Cover the bottom of an oven pan with the rosemary.

Toss the potatoes in the olive oil and place on top of the rosemary before you season them. Bake the potatoes in the oven until they are properly cooked and slightly caramelised.

Serve with pan-fried fillet.

Rack of lamb with fresh rosemary & olive oil

This falls into the 'favourite food' category. A simple meal that can hold its own in any conversation.

- 100 ml extra virgin olive oil
- 20 sprigs rosemary
- 8 lamb chops
- sea salt and freshly ground black pepper

Smear a roasting pan with olive oil, and line with all the rosemary sprigs. Layer the lamb chops onto the rosemary, season, and dribble with the rest of the olive oil. Place under a hot grill until the chops have browned. Turn over and repeat.

Serve immediately with a salad of asparagus, green beans and basil or sage. Don't hesitate to add a couple of boiled-in-the-skin baby potatoes. Fab!

Chicken with white wine, black olives & flambéed baby onions

Something really special.

- 2 T extra virgin olive oil
- 1 T butter
- 8 organic chicken thighs
- 8 organic chicken legs
- 2 T plain flour
- 125 g black olives, stoned
- 2 cloves garlic, chopped
- 500 ml white wine
- 500 ml chicken stock
- 1 bay leaf
- 4 sprigs rosemary
- 6 sage leaves, chopped
- 500 ml water
- 1 t sea salt
- freshly ground black pepper
- 24 baby onions, peeled*
- 1 T sugar
- 50 g butter
- 2 T good-quality cognac or brandy

Bring the olive oil and butter to a fast sizzle in a large pot. Brown the chicken pieces, skin-side down, until lightly crisped. Sprinkle the flour over the chicken before turning the pieces over.

Toss the olives and garlic into the pot. Add the wine and chicken stock and bring to a gentle simmer before adding the bay leaf, rosemary and sage.

Cook the chicken until tender and succulent, about 1 hour, and then spoon the meat and olives on a large, warm serving platter.

While the chicken is cooking, bring 500 ml water to the boil in a smaller pot. Add the salt and pepper. Drop the onions into the water and boil until a sharp knife slips easily into the flesh, but they are still firm. Tip out to drain, return them to the empty pot, sprinkle with the sugar, and add the butter. Cook over a moderate heat until the sugar has caramelised lightly and the onions are gloriously shiny. Have matches ready, pour the cognac over the onions and immediately light to flambée. Don't singe your eyebrows!

Pour the still flaming onions over the chicken and serve with heaps of steaming basmati rice.

* *These are really easy to peel if you first pour some boiling water over them and allow them to cool a little before slipping off the skins.*

Duck breasts with green olive tapenade

This makes for a lovely, elegant dinner … hang some lanterns in the tree.

- 75 g duck fat
- 6 shallots, peeled and finely sliced
- 4 cloves garlic, peeled and finely chopped
- 30 large green olives, stoned
- leaves from 1 bunch parsley, some sprigs thyme, and a handful sage and rosemary, chopped roughly
- 75 ml extra virgin olive oil
- 4 duck breasts, scored with a sharp knife
- 5 leeks, julienned and washed
- 250 ml duck stock or rich chicken stock
- 200 g hazelnuts, toasted, peeled and roughly chopped
- handful fresh basil to garnish

Preheat the oven to 200 deg C/Gas 6. Melt the duck fat in a frying pan and cook the shallots over a low heat with the garlic until soft but not browned. Set aside to cool.

Reserve 10 olives and purée the remainder with the cooked shallots and garlic, adding the parsley, thyme, sage, rosemary and olive oil.

Smear the herby olive tapenade over the lightly scored duck breasts, making sure to rub the mixture into the cuts you've made. Using the same pan, turn up the heat and place the breasts skin-side down to quick-fry them. The fat will start cooking immediately. Keep going until the skin is lovely and crisp. Turn and cook on the meaty side for no more than 4 minutes. You want the meat to still be succulently pink.

Remove from the pan and put aside to rest.

Deglaze the pan with a little water, blanch the leeks lightly in the pan juices, slice the remaining olives into the pan, and add the stock. Reduce until you have a rich, thick sauce. Add the hazelnuts.

To serve, thinly slice the warm duck breasts. Spoon the leek and nut mixture onto warmed serving plates, and top each with a pretty layer of sliced duck. Garnish with freshly chopped basil if you want to.

Serve with a glass of Pinot Noir.

White fish with black olives & saffron sauce

I also enjoy preparing this with tuna, but any firm fish will do.

- sea salt and freshly ground black pepper
- 6 × 200 g fish fillets
- 2 shallots, peeled and quartered
- 1 clove garlic, peeled and halved
- 200 ml olive oil
- 2 pinches saffron
- 100 ml white wine
- 200 ml chicken stock
- 20 calamata olives, stoned
- preserved lemon, thinly sliced
- handful fresh flat-leaf parsley, chopped

Preheat the oven to 180 deg C/Gas 4. Season the fish fillets. Using an ovenproof pan, lightly fry the shallots and garlic in the olive oil over a medium heat. Add the fish and gently brown.

Soak the saffron in the wine for a few minutes before pouring both the wine and the stock into the pan. Add the olives and lemon slices. Bring to a low simmer, cover and transfer to the oven for 15 minutes.

Remove the pan from the oven, place the fish fillets on a warm plate, and quickly reduce the pan juices over a high flame until lovely and saucy. Spoon over the fish, garnish with parsley, and enjoy with a heap of tiny peeled and buttered young potatoes.

Venison fillet pan-fried with ginger & sage

A great way to cook a kudu or gemsbok fillet on the stove.

- 2 T extra virgin olive oil
- 1 medium carrot, peeled and sliced in pennies
- 1 sweet brown onion, peeled and finely chopped
- 2 cloves garlic, peeled and chopped
- 100 g pancetta, diced
- 1 tiny thumb fresh ginger, peeled and chopped
- 2 small red chillies, seeded and chopped
- 1 large venison fillet, cleaned
- 2 bay leaves
- 6 sprigs parsley
- 2 T fresh sage leaves, chopped
- 4 sprigs rosemary, chopped
- 250 ml dry red wine
- salt and freshly ground black pepper to taste

Heat the olive oil in a large pan and add the carrot, onion, garlic, pancetta, ginger and chillies. Fry gently until the pancetta is browned. Add the fillet to the pan and brown properly over a low heat. This should take about 10 minutes. Add all the herbs and cook for a minute or two before removing the fillet from the pan. Deglaze with the wine, scraping all the bits from the bottom and the sides of the pan. If necessary, add some more wine and reduce the liquid until you have a lovely sauce.

Cut the fillet in portions and return to the pan to reheat in the pan juices before serving. Season and serve with all the bits and pieces spooned over the meat.

Serve with a handful of crisp rocket from your garden and a sprinkling of freshly chopped sage and parsley.

Sweet potatoes with ginger & chillies

Something zesty to add to your plate whenever you are indulging in a fillet of venison.

- 750 g sweet potatoes, peeled and cubed
- 125 ml olive oil
- 75 g butter, cut in tiny blocks
- 200 ml sugar
- 2 fingers fresh ginger, peeled and chopped
- 2 red chillies, seeded and chopped
- 6 salad onions, chopped

Place the sweet potatoes in an oven dish, drizzle with the olive oil and scatter the butter blocks over them. Bake in a hot oven, 200 deg C/Gas 6, for about an hour.

Remove the pan from the oven, drain the juices into a small pot, add the sugar, chopped ginger and chillies, and bring to the boil. You can add a little water if you do not have enough liquid.

Allow the sugar to melt and the sauce to reach a syrupy consistency.

Spoon over the still warm sweet potatoes, garnish with the salad onions and enjoy!

Chapter 2

In the Green Point Village garden

To have a dinner in our secluded garden is a feast. We light lamps next to the fountain and set out the silver and crystal, the huge antique linen napkins and the old porcelain. On a good night, when the garden is brimming with people who spill out of the alley, we have a small barbecue outside the front gate, where my son and his friends will ply arriving guests with morsels of freshly cooked lobster. There are platters of lamb ribs with lentils, or chicken with prosciutto and sage, and soft jazz music in the background. And we always invite the neighbours.

Pan-fried lamb cutlets with Gruyère

Every nervous newlywed girl needs to have one recipe she can trust for when her mother-in-law comes to dinner. My mom's was spaghetti Bolognaise … this was mine!

- 50 g butter
- 8 lamb cutlets, trimmed
- 1 onion, chopped
- 1 T flour
- 200 ml dry white wine
- 2 t smooth mustard
- 100 ml lamb stock
- 125 g Gruyère, grated*
- 1 small gherkin, finely chopped
- sea salt and freshly ground black pepper

Melt the butter and fry the cutlets in a warm pan on the stove until the fat is crispy. Do not overcook the meat. Medium-rare to medium is fine.

Remove the meat from the pan and keep warm. Fry the onion in the pan juices until soft.

Mix the flour into some of the wine and add to the pan with the rest of the wine, mustard and the stock. Stir until the sauce has thickened. Allow to simmer a little before adding the grated cheese and gherkin. Stir until the cheese has melted. Taste and season. Spoon the sauce over the cutlets and serve.

You'll never want lamb cutlets cooked any other way!

* A mature cheddar is really good as well!

Lamb ribs with lentils & prosciutto

If you are able to find them, try puy lentils – they are truly lovely.

- 1½ kg lamb ribs, cut in half and French trimmed*
- 100 g butter
- 100 ml dry white wine
- few sprigs thyme
- 4 cloves garlic
- 1½ ℓ veal stock
- 12 baby onions, peeled
- 6 young carrots, peeled
- sea salt and freshly ground black pepper

Trim away any excess fat from the meat.

Melt 60 g of the butter in a deep pan, and sear the ribs over a high heat; then add the wine, thyme and garlic. Bring to a gentle boil and simmer until the alcohol has evaporated. You will smell when it has all gone! Add the stock and bring back to a gentle simmer.

Cover and allow to simmer for about 2 hours, checking regularly that the stew does not cook dry (if things start to look serious, top up with a little more stock or water).

Meanwhile, melt the rest of the butter, and braise the baby onions until tender and glossy.

Add the onions and carrots to the stew, and cook for another 15 minutes before removing the lamb and vegetables from the pan.

Spoon on a serving dish and keep warm.

Scoop most of the fat from the cooking liquid, and then bring it to a vigorous boil, reducing it to a sauce-like consistency. Season to taste with freshly ground black pepper and sea salt, then spoon it over the lamb ribs.

Serve with lentils and prosciutto (see overleaf).

* Ask your butcher to French trim the lamb ribs.

Puy lentils with prosciutto

- 6 thin slices prosciutto, cut into narrow strips
- 50 ml extra virgin olive oil
- 500 g puy lentils, cooked
- sea salt and freshly ground black pepper
- thyme for garnish

Fry the prosciutto in the olive oil, then fold into the cooked lentils. Season after tasting. Garnish with freshly cut sprigs of thyme.

Chicken with prosciutto & sage

Serves 6

You can use any kind of bird for this recipe – I love using quails and then I place the prosciutto and sage into the cavity of the little birds.

- 1 chicken
- 18 thin slices prosciutto
- 12 sage leaves plus a sprig for garnish
- 50 ml extra virgin olive oil
- 2 red onions, peeled and roughly sliced
- 2 cloves garlic
- 2 small carrots, peeled
- bouquet garni
- 300 ml chicken stock
- 300 ml of a serious red wine

Remove the rather oily pope's nose from the chicken. Place 6 slices of prosciutto and the sage into the cavity of the bird, and then truss the chicken with a piece of string.

Cover the bottom of a large heavy-based pot with olive oil and fry the onions until slightly caramelised.

Add the bird and lightly brown on both sides. Add the garlic, carrots, bouquet garni – add the last 6 sage leaves to the latter – and remaining prosciutto, and fry together for about 5 minutes.

Pour the stock and wine into the pot and bring to a slow simmer. Gently cook over a relatively low heat until the meat is almost falling off the bones.

Remove the chicken from the pot and keep warm. If necessary, reduce the sauce to thicken. Season and pour over the chicken. Garnish with a sprig of sage and serve with some creamy polenta.

Seared tuna with pistou, tomatoes & black olives

Ideally one would throw these wonderful thickly cut tuna fillets onto an open grill.

- 4 × 250 g fresh tuna steaks, thickly cut
- flesh of 4 ripe tomatoes, peeled and seeded
- 20 black olives, stoned

Pistou
- 3 cloves garlic
- leaves from 1 bunch basil
- 100 ml extra virgin olive oil
- 8 anchovies

With this dish, it is necessary to prepare the pistou* first. Place the garlic, basil, olive oil and anchovies in a food processor and blend to a rough paste. Grill the fish at a very high heat until it is completely seared on all sides but still pink and succulent inside.

Spoon the pistou into a small bowl, add the tomatoes and olives, and gently fold together.

Place the smoking-hot fish on individual plates and spoon the pistou mixture over the fish. Serve immediately with a green salad.

* *A pistou is a cold sauce often made by pounding the ingredients together using a mortar and pestle – but the food processor does a good job of it too.*

Roast chicken with green olives & prunes

This is a wonderful dish that I often serve at big, friendly gatherings. It's equally great at room temperature.

- 125 ml extra virgin olive oil
- 2 heads garlic
- 50 ml balsamic vinegar
- 75 ml dried oregano
- 300 g prunes, stoned
- 300 g green olives, stoned
- 250 ml white wine
- 125 ml capers
- 5 free-range chickens, portioned
- 125 ml coriander, chopped

The day before, pour a little olive oil over the garlic heads, wrap them in foil and bake them in a warm oven at 180 deg C/Gas 4 for 15 minutes or until soft. Squeeze the garlic out of the peels and whisk into the rest of the olive oil and the balsamic vinegar. Add the oregano, prunes, olives, white wine and capers. Put the chicken portions in a layer in a big oven dish and season.

Spoon over the garlic mixture, cover and refrigerate overnight.

Heat the oven to 180 deg C/Gas 4, cover the dish with a lid of foil, and bake for about an hour or until the chicken is well cooked. Arrange on a lovely platter, and spoon the olives, capers and prunes over the food using a slotted spoon. Garnish with the chopped coriander and serve.

Fennel chicken cooked on a spit

This slow-roasted chicken with its smell of sage and garlic is truly lovely served by moonlight.

- 2 chickens, deboned
- 20 thin slices prosciutto
- 250 g pancetta – 1 piece
- 250 g prosciutto – 1 piece
- 6 cloves garlic
- 20 g sage leaves (dried) or 20 fresh leaves
- 2 t fennel seeds
- seasoning

After deboning the chickens, leaving all the meat attached to the skin, tuck in the meat of the legs and the wings and place the chickens, skin down, on top of the prosciutto slices. Coarsely chop the pancetta, prosciutto, garlic and sage all together. Transfer to a bowl and add the fennel seeds and seasoning. Spoon the chopped ingredients onto the prepared chickens. Roll the chickens with the prosciutto slices into tight rolls and tie each with 5 pieces of string.

Thread onto a skewer and fit onto a spit. Cook for about 1 hour. Remove from the spit and let it rest for 10 minutes before untying and discarding the string. Serve immediately with oven-baked potatoes with sage.

Roast chicken with saffron, hazelnuts & honey

Serves 4

Turn a good old roast chicken into a great dish … and don't under-estimate what that pinch of saffron will do.

- 2 onions, roughly chopped
- 4 T olive oil
- 1 t ground ginger
- 1 t ground cinnamon
- generous pinch of saffron strands
- juice of 1 lemon
- 4 T coarse sea salt
- 1 t black pepper
- 1 large chicken, quartered
- 70 g honey
- 100 g hazelnuts, chopped and lightly roasted
- 2 spring onions, roughly chopped

In a large bowl, mix the onions, olive oil, ginger, cinnamon, saffron, lemon juice, salt and pepper. Spoon over the chicken pieces and allow to rest for about an hour.

Preheat the oven to 190 deg C/Gas 5. Roast the chicken in a large enough oven dish. The pieces should be arranged skin-side up and roasted, covered, for about 55 minutes or until cooked. While the chicken is roasting, mix the honey and nuts together to make a rough paste. Remove the chicken from the oven and spoon a generous amount of nut paste onto each piece. Return to the oven for 5 to 10 minutes, until the chicken is cooked through and the nuts are golden brown.

Transfer the chicken to a serving dish and garnish with chopped spring onions.

Chapter 3

On the Food Studio stoep

Seated around the huge slate table, which hails from the stony hills around Sutherland, we have a bird's-eye view of Cape Town Stadium. We can also see the Mouille Point Lighthouse at the far end of the walkway through the park. On misty evenings, we listen to the low tones of the foghorn warning ships from the treacherous Cape shores. On the menu will be the succulent duck with pears that my dear friend Heather introduced me to and a bottle or two of Pinot Noir.

Fish with a herb & wine marinade

This is particularly great with both yellowtail and tuna, but works with almost all line fish.

- handful sprigs rosemary, chopped
- 1 sprig fennel, chopped
- 8 sprigs flat-leaf parsley, chopped
- 100 ml dry white wine
- juice of 1 large lemon
- 1 t sugar
- 3 cloves garlic, crushed
- 250 ml olive oil
- 2 bay leaves
- 6 pieces line fish
- salt and freshly ground black pepper
- 1 T cream (optional)

Put the fresh herbs into a blender along with the wine, lemon juice, sugar, garlic and 175 ml olive oil. Liquidise. Add the bay leaves.

Dry the fish fillets and season them. Pour some of the marinade into a flat dish, put the fish fillets into the mixture and pour the rest over the fish. Leave for at least an hour.

Drain the fish. Heat the remainder of the oil. Fry the fish until done. Remove from the pan and keep warm. Add the marinade to the pan and reduce by half. Strain the sauce, add cream if you want to, pour over the fish and serve.

Heather's roasted ginger & thyme duck

My friend Heather served this one evening on her rooftop patio … unforgettable! I had to bribe her to get the recipe.

- 2 ducks (about 1,5 kg each)
- seasoning
- 150 g fresh ginger, sliced
- 2 leeks, sliced
- 2 carrots, chopped in large chunks
- 4 cloves garlic
- 20 sprigs thyme
- 4 firm pears, halved and peeled
- 250 ml red wine
- 250 ml chicken stock

Rinse the ducks and pat dry with a paper towel. Season with sea salt and ground black pepper. Combine the ginger, leeks, carrots, garlic and thyme, and use this to stuff the ducks. Place the ducks on the rack of a roasting pan, and pour water into the pan to just below the level of the rack. Cover tightly with foil and roast/steam for 45 minutes at 220 deg C/Gas 7.

Remove from the oven and turn the oven down to 200 deg C/Gas 6. Remove the foil, pour the liquid into a bowl and set the liquid to cool. Return the ducks to the oven and roast uncovered for another 45 minutes. They are ready when they are crisp and a lovely caramel colour. In the meantime, peel and core the pears. Skim some of the duck fat off the bowl and into a pan, and braise the pears in the fat over medium heat for 5 minutes. Remove from the pan, sprinkle with black pepper, and keep both pears and pan aside.

Remove the ducks from the oven, scoop out the stuffing and add it to the pan, along with the red wine. Set the ducks aside to rest, and bring the contents of the pan to a rapid boil. Let the liquid reduce by half, scoop out the solids, add the chicken stock, and reduce again to the saucy, yummy stage … if you don't know what that looks like, call me.

Arrange a breast, leg and thigh per serving on mashed potatoes, pasta or couscous; add a pear to each serving.

Pour the reduced sauce over the dish and garnish with thyme.

Deboned, stuffed quail

Search high and low for these little birds if you have to … I promise it will be worth your while.

- 50 ml extra virgin olive oil
- 300 g artichoke hearts, sliced
- 150 g green olives, stoned and sliced
- 2 sundried peppadews, sliced
- 3 cloves garlic, chopped
- 50 g chives, chopped
- 125 g cashew nuts, grilled
- 250 g chèvre, sliced
- 6 quails, deboned
- sea salt and freshly ground black pepper

Heat the olive oil in a pot and add the artichokes, olives, peppadews, garlic, chives and cashew nuts. Mix over the heat, remove from the stove and fold the cheese into the mixture.

Using a tablespoon, fill the cavity of each quail with the stuffing, and place the quails, legs and wingtips up, on a baking tray. Smear them with the remnants of the oil in the pot. Season and bake at 180 deg C/Gas 4 for around 35 minutes, or until the juices run clear when pricked with a sharp knife. Serve the quails with polenta or couscous and a helping of baby green beans with garlic butter.

Chicken with peaches, honey & parsley

Serves 4 or 6, depending on the size of the chicken

In summertime, there is never a shortage of yellow cling peaches ... try this one.

- 100 ml extra virgin olive oil
- 1 chicken, cut up into portions
- 25 ml paprika
- 50 ml flour, seasoned with salt and pepper
- 1 celery stick, chopped
- 6 leeks, chopped
- 3 cloves garlic, chopped
- 250 ml chicken stock
- 250 ml orange juice
- 4 peaches, peeled and sliced
- 50 ml honey
- ½ bunch parsley, chopped

Heat the olive oil in a pot, and fry the chicken pieces until brown. Dust with paprika and seasoned flour. Add the celery, leeks and garlic, and fry lightly. Add the liquids and simmer for 35 minutes or until the chicken pieces are soft.

Remove the chicken and reduce the stock until it becomes a thick sauce. Add the peaches and honey, season and serve with rice. Garnish with parsley.

Chicken with pancetta, preserved lemon & herbs

For a lovely change, use prosciutto instead of pancetta.

- 125 ml extra virgin olive oil
- 1 T butter, plus 2 extra teaspoons
- 6 chicken drumsticks
- 6 chicken thighs
- 2 preserved lemons, sliced
- 500 ml white wine
- 250 ml chicken stock
- 250 ml each parsley, rosemary and sage, chopped
- 12 slices pancetta
- freshly ground black pepper to taste
- crusty white bread to serve

Melt the olive oil and the tablespoon of butter together in a large pot. Brown the chicken pieces gently, and then add the lemon pieces. Pour the wine over, cover with the lid and bring to the boil. After three minutes, add the stock and herbs. Bring back to a slow simmer.

Meanwhile, pan-fry the slices of pancetta in the remaining butter until crisp, then add to the simmering pot.

Allow to gently cook for about 45 minutes, then season with freshly ground pepper. Serve when the chicken is succulently tender, and scoop up the tangy sauce with the crusty white bread.

French lamb shanks with tomatoes & cream cheese

The French use orange peel with their lamb dishes. What a refreshing taste!

- 6 lamb shanks
- 1 carrot, peeled and sliced into pennies
- 1 celery stick, chopped
- 1 whole garlic bulb, halved and dribbled with 2 T extra virgin olive oil
- bouquet garni
- 1 red onion, peeled and chopped
- 5 ripe tomatoes, peeled, seeded and chopped
- zest of 1 orange
- 500 ml dry white wine
- salt and freshly ground black pepper
- puff pastry, thawed
- 1 t butter
- 1 pear, cubed
- 6 T cream cheese
- gremolata*

Preheat the oven to 180 deg C/Gas 4. Arrange the shanks in a deep baking dish and add the carrot, celery, garlic, bouquet garni, onion, tomatoes and zest. Pour the wine over and season. Cover and bake for 3 hours, until the meat is as soft as marrow.

In the meantime, cut the pastry into 6 cm × 8 cm rounds and place on a greased baking tray. About 20 minutes before the shanks are due to come out, pop the pastry rounds into the oven as well and bake until puffed and golden brown.

Melt the butter in a small frying pan and toss in the cubed pear until it is slightly caramelised but still crunchy.

Make a hollow in each round of pastry and place each in the centre of a plate.

Spoon some cubed pear and a dollop of cream cheese into the hollow. Add a hot shank to each, and spoon some cooking juices over and around the shanks.

Sprinkle with gremolata, loosen the roasted garlic cloves from the bulb, and use to garnish. Serve with a fabulous Cabernet Sauvignon.

* To make the gremolata, mix 3 T finely chopped parsley, 1 T finely chopped garlic, 1 T finely chopped lemon zest and 1 T finely chopped orange zest together. Set aside until needed.

Stuffed lamb shoulder

Serves 6

This is truly lovely and surprisingly easy to prepare.

- 100 g pork belly
- 1 small onion
- 1 t dried thyme leaves
- 50 g black olives, chopped
- 50 ml brandy
- salt and pepper
- 1 boned lamb shoulder
- 3 sprigs rosemary
- 1 celery stick, with leaves, chopped
- olive oil
- 1 bay leaf

Finely dice the pork belly. Peel and dice the onion, mix it with the diced meat, and add the thyme, chopped olives and brandy. Season with salt and freshly ground black pepper, and taste. Stuff the lamb shoulder, spreading the stuffing over the whole surface. Chop the rosemary and celery stick, and add the herbs. Roll up the breast, tie it up, brush it with olive oil and season gently. Place the bay leaf in the pan with the meat.

Cook in a 180 deg C/Gas 4 oven for 1 hour.

Chapter 4

On the Victorian balcony

Dinner on the Victorian balcony is always a lovely, gentle affair. We switch on the small table lamp and put pillows on the chairs. Maybe a vase of poppies. Veal with salsa verde and small carrots with walnuts are perfect as we chat about the week gone by. The walls of the old home where we have lived for more than 20 years join in the conversation about remembered joys and lives, and hopeful plans for the next day, week, month.

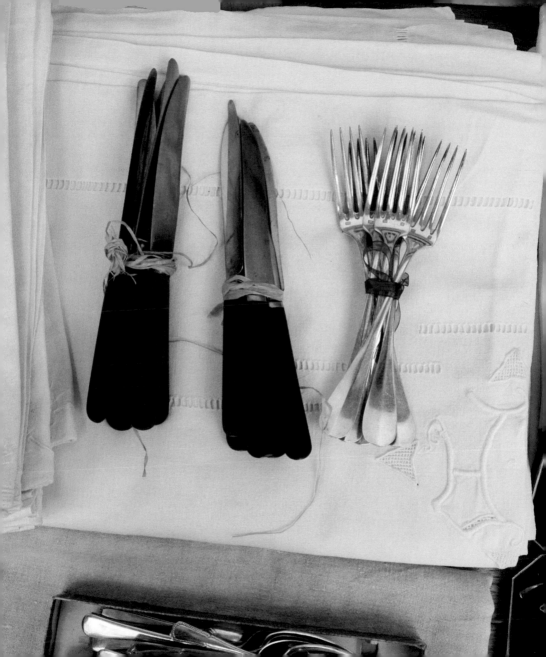

Beef tongue with caper berries & black olives

Serves 4

This was one of those accidental recipes that just happened when some friends arrived unexpectedly. It's delicious though, and I've repeated it often.

- 1 beef tongue, cooked,* peeled and sliced into thinnish slivers
- 250 ml cream
- 2 t honey
- 1 T walnut oil
- 1 T smooth French mustard
- 100 g caper berries
- 250 g black olives, stoned

Place the slices of beef tongue on a serving platter, allowing them to overlap slightly. Keep warm.

In a small mixing bowl, whisk together the cream, honey, walnut oil and mustard. It will blend into a yummy, thick sauce. Scatter the caper berries and olives over the slices of tongue before spooning the sauce over the still warm meat.

Serve immediately with some fruity white wine.

* To cook a pickled beef tongue, you need a large pot with enough water to cover the meat comfortably. Add a glass of dry white wine to the water just for effect ... and drink one! Add about 6 cloves to the water, as well as a bay leaf or two. A few whole peppercorns aren't a bad idea either.

Bring the liquid to a slow boil and keep that going until the meat is absolutely tender. About 2 hours should do it. Allow the meat to cool down slightly before peeling it. You don't want to burn your fingers!

Fish with tomato & olive sauce

Enough to spoon generously over 6 portions

This light, fresh sauce is wonderful with fish.

- 250 g small black olives, stoned
- 100 ml olive oil
- 50 ml lemon juice
- 2 t coriander seeds, lightly crushed
- handful sage leaves
- 2 ripe tomatoes, skinned, seeded and chopped

Heat the olives gently in the oil, and then squeeze in the lemon juice. Remove from the heat and add the coriander and sage. Finally, stir in the tomatoes, and spoon over the cooked fish fillets. Serve immediately.

Chicken with tomatoes & baby onions

One of my favourite recipes from my mother's kitchen.

- 100 ml extra virgin olive oil
- 150 ml plain white flour
- 60 ml paprika
- sea salt and freshly ground black pepper
- 1 free-range chicken, portioned
- 20 small baby onions, peeled
- 2 green peppers, grilled, peeled and seeded
- 2 cloves garlic, peeled and chopped
- 5 very ripe tomatoes, peeled and seeded
- 50 ml salted butter
- 20 small fresh mushrooms
- fresh parsley and basmati rice to serve

Heat the olive oil in a flameproof casserole. Mix the flour, paprika and seasoning, and sieve over the chicken pieces. Brown them. Add the baby onions to the casserole with the chicken. Slice the green peppers in strips and add to the pot.

Add the garlic. Slice the tomatoes in strips over a bowl to catch the juices, and add it all to the casserole. Do remember to remove the tomato pips ... they are the culprits that can cause a tomato and chicken casserole to go sour. Add enough water to allow for some happy simmering – cooking should take just about an hour.

While that's going on, melt the butter in a pan and allow it to brown to make beurre noisette or nut butter. Add the mushrooms, and fry until they have caramelised.

To serve, pour the mushrooms over the dish, and garnish with a handful of freshly picked parsley. Have basmati rice on the side.

Veal cutlets with salsa verde

Veal cutlets are sometimes difficult to come by ... convince your butcher to make a plan.

- 6 veal cutlets
- handful thyme leaves
- juice and rind of 1 lemon
- 125 ml dry white wine
- 300 ml extra virgin olive oil
- sea salt and freshly ground black pepper
- 1 bunch flat-leaf parsley, stems picked off
- 20 fresh basil leaves
- 20 small, crisp rocket leaves
- 1 clove garlic
- 6 anchovy fillets
- 1 T capers

Trim some of the fat from the cutlets ... but leave a little; it really adds flavour. Place them in a large dish and sprinkle with the thyme, lemon juice and rind, wine and 100 ml of the olive oil. Season lightly. Cover and leave to marinate for at least an hour, though two hours is better.

To make the salsa verde, put the parsley, basil, rocket, garlic, anchovies and capers in a food processor and blend to a smooth paste. Add the remaining olive oil in a steady stream, continuing until emulsified.

Pat the meat dry and cook over a high heat in a very warm, oiled griddle pan. I love those little stripes ... they make the dish look wildly professional!

Place one cutlet per person on a warmed plate, season, and spoon a dollop of fragrant salsa verde over the meat.

This dish needs a gentle Bordeaux.

Carrots with roasted walnuts in orange juice

Serves 4

This is possibly the most wonderful taste surprise I've ever had.

- 2 large, ripe oranges
- 300 g fresh baby carrots, peeled
- 100 g walnuts, chopped
- 50 g butter
- sea salt and freshly ground black pepper to taste

Thinly zest one of the oranges. Squeeze the juice from both. Place the carrots, nuts and zest in an ovenproof casserole and pour the juice over. Dot the carrots with the butter and season lightly. Cover and bake at 180 deg C/Gas 4 for 45 minutes, or until tender.

Serve with any white meat.

Creamy chicken with rosemary

Serves 4

This is one of those comfortable dishes one makes when one's feeling slightly low and in need of some nurturing.

- 2 T extra virgin olive oil
- 50 g butter
- 1 medium chicken, cut in portions
- 1 stick celery, washed and chopped (leaves and all)
- 2 leeks, sliced in pennies and washed
- 6 long sprigs rosemary, rolled tightly in two leek leaves
- 500 ml chicken stock
- 250 ml cream
- 50 ml dry sherry
- salt and freshly ground black pepper

Heat the olive oil in a pan; melt the butter into it and quick-fry the chicken until lightly browned.

Add the celery, leeks, rosemary and stock. Allow the broth to simmer gently until the chicken is cooked to perfection – almost falling off the bone. And please add more stock if it is needed! Remove the chicken from the pan and keep warm.

Add the cream and reduce the sauce until it is lovely and thick. Remove the rosemary bouquet garni. Stir the sherry into the cream sauce, pour over the chicken, season to taste and garnish with a fresh sprig of rosemary.

Utterly satisfying.

Beef fillet

There are many ways to prepare a fillet – this really is one of the best ...

- 1 x 3 kg fillet of beef
- 75 g butter
- 15 ml sea salt
- freshly ground black pepper to taste
- 75 g celery, chopped
- 75 g carrot, peeled and chopped
- 2 T flat-leaf parsley, chopped
- 1 small onion, peeled and chopped
- 2 small leeks, sliced in pennies and washed
- 1 T lemon zest
- 2 cloves garlic, peeled and crushed
- 350 ml fresh cream
- 350 ml sour cream

Rub the meat with some of the butter and season. Heat the leftover butter in a large cooking pan. Add the celery, carrot, parsley, onion, leeks, lemon zest and garlic to the pan. Place the beef on top of the other ingredients in the pan and roast in a moderate oven, 180 deg C/Gas 4, for about 25 minutes until it is cooked but still rare. Baste the meat with the vegetable mixture before putting it on a warm platter. Keep warm. Strain the vegetables from the juices and remove most of the fat.

Pour the pan juices into a small cooking pot, add the fresh cream and reduce until really thick. Add the sour cream and warm thoroughly without bringing to a boil. Slice the meat into thick slices, and spoon the sauce over the meat.

I really enjoy the combination of small jacket potatoes and ripe avocado with the fillet.

Utterly delicious with a glass of Shiraz.

Chapter 5

In the Food Studio kitchen

The Food Studio is where I create and teach. Where I wrestle with enormous piles of produce, and serve the droves of people who move through my life and kitchen. What a privilege to prepare all my favourite country dishes, most of them with a solid taste of the Auvergne, for all of you!

Rabbit with creamy chestnuts, tripe with white wine, a good old cassoulet and a real chef's entrecôte. Fabulous, real food.

Leg of lamb with anchovies, garlic & rosemary

This is a remarkably subtle and beautiful combination. Do not be put off by the quantities of garlic. When cooked, it is a gentle purée.

- 1 leg of lamb
- 500 g garlic, about a third of it peeled and cut in slivers, and the rest left whole
- 9 anchovy fillets, halved
- 18 sprigs rosemary
- olive oil
- salt and pepper
- 175 ml lamb stock

Make 18 small slits in the lamb, and stuff each with a sliver of garlic, half an anchovy and a sprig of rosemary.

Preheat your oven to 200 deg C/Gas 6. Place a roasting rack in a roasting pan, put the meat uncovered on top of the rack and roast for 1 hour. The meat should be cooked but still slightly pink in the middle when you slice it.

While the meat is cooking, blanch the rest of the garlic cloves in boiling water for about 5 minutes. Drain, wrap in a piece of foil onto which you've smeared some olive oil, season, and put in the oven with the lamb for 30 minutes. Remove the garlic from the oven. Squeeze the now fabulously soft purée out of the cloves into a saucepan and add the lamb stock. If there are any pan juices in the roasting pan, add those as well. Gently reduce the sauce until it has a thick, creamy consistency.

Serve the sliced leg on a large platter with baby potatoes in the skin. And, of course, serious amounts of the garlic cream!

Tripe & trotters with white wine

I've travelled far for a bowl of tripe in my life, but realised it would probably be more economical to just do my own ... This is good.

- 150 ml duck fat
- 2 whole sheep tripe, cleaned
- 8 trotters, cleaned
- 750 ml good-quality white wine
- 500 ml chicken stock
- 2 carrots, peeled and sliced
- 3 leeks, peeled and sliced
- 6 cloves garlic, peeled
- 1 whole celery stick, rinsed and sliced
- 1 bouquet garni with fresh sage leaves added

Heat the fat in a large casserole, and fry the tripe lightly for about 3 minutes ... it's all about getting the rich flavour of the duck fat incorporated. Add the trotters, then the wine, and bring to the boil before pouring in the chicken stock. Add the carrots, leeks, garlic, celery and bouquet garni. Bring to a slow simmer and keep it simmering for about 2 hours. Add more liquid if necessary.

When the tripe is soft, remove from the casserole and cut with a pair of scissors into small, bite-sized pieces. Return to the pot. Remove the trotters from the casserole, and debone and shred the meat. Return the meat to the casserole. Reduce the liquid to a lovely, thick sauce before you serve the tripe on basmati rice with a dollop of aioli or basil pesto. Garnish with persillade.

Rabbit in red wine with chestnuts

We should eat rabbit more often. It is healthy ... and delicious too!

- 50 ml olive oil
- 6 leeks, sliced into pennies and washed
- 500 g pork belly, cut into thin slices
- 2 carrots, peeled and roughly chopped
- 2 rabbits, cut into 6 pieces each
- 750 ml red wine
- 750 ml chicken stock
- 1 bouquet garni with lots of sage
- 2 cloves garlic, chopped
- 25 ml freshly ground black pepper
- 500 g chestnuts
- sea salt

Heat the olive oil in a heavy-bottomed pot and sauté the leeks. Add the pork belly and fry until browned. Add the carrots and then the rabbit. Brown the meat properly before adding the wine. Let it simmer until the alcohol has evaporated ... you will smell when it's gone! Add the stock, bouquet garni, garlic and pepper. Simmer until the meat is done, about 1½ hours.

Remove the rabbit from the pot, reduce the lovely stock until it has a thick, glossy consistency, then add the chestnuts. Taste the sauce and, if necessary, add some salt. Then gently reintroduce the rabbit pieces to the pot to reheat. Serve immediately with small white potatoes.

Vegetables with persillade

- baby artichokes
- little onions, peeled and par-boiled in salted water
- unpeeled garlic cloves
- bouquet garni
- 100 ml butter, salted
- chiffonade of lettuce, cut up 'kerk-basaar' style in thin strips

Preheat the oven to 180 deg C/Gas 4. Put the artichokes, onions, garlic and bouquet garni into an oven dish, and cover with a lid or a sheet of foil. Sweat for about 30 minutes and remove from the oven. In the meantime, heat some butter in a pan and add the chiffonade of lettuce to the butter. Give it a quick swirl before adding it, with the butter, to the vegetables. Just before serving, you can add any of the following vegetables to the dish: diced little green beans, lightly braised; broccoli florets, parboiled; small courgettes, julienned and sautéed; or raw peas.

Vegetables that have been sweated in butter can be finished by swirling in a little double cream, off the heat. Serve this scattered with a persillade – mix together a bunch of flat-leaf parsley, roughly chopped, and the zest of 2 lemons.

Cassoulet

This is a truly authentic French country recipe ... one to die for.

- 500 g Tarbais beans (big white ones)
- 250 g salted pork belly
- 2 big onions, each studded with 4 cloves
- 1 bouquet garni
- 6 cloves garlic, peeled
- 1 carrot, peeled
- 1 saucisson à cuire (this type of sausage is boiled in a liquid; it is 100% pork)
- 2 T duck fat, plus extra for frying*
- 500 g pork shoulder, cut into medium-sized cubes
- ¾ ℓ chicken stock
- 40 g flour
- 4 ripe tomatoes, peeled and chopped really finely
- salt and freshly ground pepper
- 4 saucisses de Toulouse (pork also, just smaller and they need to be fried)
- 500 g confit de canard**
- breadcrumbs

The day before, put the beans in unsalted cold water.

The next day, boil the beans, pork belly, onions with cloves, bouquet garni, garlic cloves and carrot. Water must truly cover everything. Boil slowly for 1½ hours (taste the beans).

Twenty minutes before the beans are ready, add the saucisson to the boiling beans.

Melt 2 big tablespoons of duck fat and brown the cubes of pork shoulder until golden brown, then take them out of the casserole. In the casserole, prepare a roux brun with the stock and the flour. Add the tomato pulp.

Add salt and pepper (not too much salt), put back the pork shoulder cubes and allow the dish to simmer for 2 hours.

Brown the saucisses de Toulouse in a tiny bit of duck fat.

In the oven, heated to around 200 deg C/Gas 6, lay the pieces of confit on the 'grille' (my source could not find any other word to describe the oven shelf) until they lose their fat and become crispy (about 20 minutes). Strain the beans and keep the jus de cuisson (use as a stock).

Cut the saucisson in big slices. Set up a terracotta dish with the beans and all the meat on top, and

continues overleaf

cover with the roux brun and a little of the saved stock. See if there is enough seasoning. Sprinkle the breadcrumbs on top and cook in the oven au gratin.

Finish the cassoulet, lay on your bed and refuse to eat for two days!!!

It can be prepared the day before and cooked au gratin before serving.

*   duck fat: used to preserve and cook food. Can be found at some of our delis, or make your own!

** confit de canard: duck cooked in its own fat and stored in a pot, covered in the same fat to preserve it.

Poulet à la Lyonnaise

A classic Parisian bistro dish.

- 250 g tomatoes, peeled, seeded and chopped
- 1 large chicken
- 125 ml butter
- 2 T flour
- sea salt and freshly ground black pepper
- 1 T white wine vinegar
- 125 ml dry white wine
- 175 ml fresh cream
- baby potatoes, peeled and steamed, to serve
- 4 cloves garlic, chopped, to serve
- 1 T butter, melted, to serve

Cook the tomatoes in a small pot for about 10 minutes. Remove from the heat and keep warm.

Cut the chicken into eight pieces. Heat the butter in a saucepan. Toss the chicken pieces in the flour and drop into the hot butter. Brown lightly on all sides, then lower the heat, cover and cook slowly for 15 minutes. Season.

Add the vinegar to the pan, and scrape around the bottom to lift all the sticky bits. Then add the wine and stir well. Add the cream and the tomatoes. Mix well, cover and allow to simmer for about 10 minutes or until the chicken is cooked through. Taste and season.

Serve hot with gently steamed baby potatoes.

Garnish them with a handful of freshly chopped raw garlic stirred into the tablespoon of melted butter.

Succulent duck with ginger, chillies & coconut milk

I once found a photograph of this dish with half of the recipe torn off. So I had to reinvent it ... enjoy!

- 1 T duck fat
- 1 duck, cut into 8 portions*
- 4 shallots, peeled and chopped
- 4 cloves garlic, peeled and chopped
- 4 fresh red chillies, seeded and chopped
- 2 t fresh ginger
- 1 t turmeric
- 4 cardamon pods, husked and ground
- 1 stem fresh lemongrass, chopped
- 2 ℓ coconut milk
- sea salt and freshly ground black pepper to taste
- basmati rice to serve

Melt the fat in a large pot, add the duck pieces, and fry over a medium heat until brown. Add the shallots, garlic, chillies, ginger, turmeric, cardamon and lemongrass. Stir-fry gently for about 2 minutes before adding the coconut milk. Bring to a gentle boil and simmer for at least 90 minutes, until the meat is deliciously tender and the sauce wonderfully thick.

Taste and season.

Spoon the duck and sauce onto a warm serving platter and serve with basmati rice.

I enjoy a chilled Sauvignon Blanc with this dish.

* *Wash the duck portions in cold water and rub each with white wine vinegar. Pour boiling water over them and leave to stand for 5 minutes. The vinegar removes the slightly wild odour, and the boiling water melts some excess fat under the skin. Drain the meat in a colander and pat dry before you start to cook.*

Venison in red wine & chocolate sauce

Serves 10 if you're using the leg and 6 if you're using the shoulder

I love using wild boar in this old Italian recipe, but leg or shoulder of venison works equally well.

Marinade

- 100 ml olive oil
- 125 g diced pork belly
- 2 carrots, peeled and sliced
- 2 leeks, sliced and rinsed
- 1 t dried sage
- 3 bay leaves
- 1 bouquet garni
- 4 cloves garlic, chopped
- 750 ml good-quality red wine

Marinade

Heat the olive oil in a large casserole and gently fry the pork belly until the fat runs. Add the carrots and the leeks and cook them gently. Add the herbs and the garlic and heat through. Add the wine and bring to a gentle boil. Allow the alcohol to evaporate … you will smell when it's all gone! It takes about 5 minutes.

Remove the liquid from the heat and let it cool down completely before you use it.

Place the venison in a huge lidded container.

Pour the cooled marinade over the meat and cover.

Turn the meat every 12 hours for 48 hours.

continues overleaf

Casserole

- 100 ml olive oil
- 1 carrot, peeled and sliced
- 1 leek, peeled and chopped
- 1,25 kg venison, trimmed
- 1 t dried sage
- 2 cloves garlic, chopped
- 2 bay leaves
- 1 bouquet garni
- 750 ml good-quality red wine
- 100 g dark chocolate, grated
- 125 ml cream
- 125 g pine nuts, roasted
- 250 g dried brandy-soaked prunes*

Remove the pips from the prunes and put them into a jar. Fill the jar with excellent brandy – you should not have any other kind in your cupboard! – before sealing the jar. Let the prunes soak for at least 5 days before you need to use them.

Casserole

Heat the olive oil in a casserole that is big enough to hold the whole piece of venison. Fry the carrot and leek. When you're ready to cook, remove the venison from the marinade, and dry with absorbent paper.

Pour the marinade through a sieve and keep the liquid.

Seal the venison on all sides in the hot olive oil before adding the sage, garlic, bay leaves and bouquet garni. Pour the strained marinade and red wine over the meat. Bring the liquid to a steady boil and simmer for about 2 hours. The liquid should be reduced by half and the meat soft. Remove the meat from the heat, put it on a platter and let it rest before slicing it thinly.

Bring the liquid to a fast boil and reduce until it has a thick, saucy consistency. Turn the heat down and stir the grated chocolate into the sauce. Add the cream and the pine nuts. Add the prunes to the sauce and allow it to heat through. Spoon the sauce over the meat. Serve with polenta.

Entrecôte Beaujolaise

If you have ever wondered how classically trained chefs 'do' a steak ... here you go!

- 2 T olive oil
- 2 sirloin steaks
- 2 T butter
- 2 shallots, peeled and finely chopped
- 125 ml dry white wine
- sea salt and freshly ground black pepper to taste
- flat-leaf parsley, chopped

Heat the oil in a frying pan. Sear the steaks quickly on both sides. Lower the heat and cook as required ... preferably rare! Remove from the pan and keep warm.

Pour off the oil from the pan and toss in 1 T butter. When it's melted and 'hot', fry the shallots until golden. Pour in the wine and reduce by half.

Remove from the heat and incorporate the leftover butter in walnut-sized bits, stirring well after each knob has melted away.

Pour the sauce over the steaks, season, and garnish with parsley. Accompany with a fabulously creamy baked potato and a dollop of sour cream.

A glass of serious Cabernet Sauvignon will complement your meal well.

Veal kidneys in mustard sauce

Serves 4

Good mustard can make such a difference to any meal!

- 1 T olive oil
- 500 g veal kidneys, sliced into bite-sized pieces
- 1 T butter
- 2 shallots, finely chopped
- 2 T brandy
- 150 ml thick cream
- 1 T creamy mustard
- salt and freshly ground black pepper

Heat the olive oil in a frying pan until really warm. Put the kidneys in the pan and sauté for about 6 minutes until they are lightly browned. Take care not to overcook them. Lift them from the pan with a spoon and keep in a warm dish.

Add the butter to the juices in the pan and heat well before adding the shallots for a quick sauté. Turn up the heat, add the brandy and simmer until the juice has reduced by half.

Add the cream and the mustard as well as the kidneys to the pan and gently reheat them. Taste, season and serve immediately.

Chapter 6

In front of the fireplace

Winter in the Cape is a time of wet pavements, shiny and dripping branches, and icy winds. Also of wood fires in Adam fireplaces, bottles of red wine, long conversations and bowls of comfort food.

It's a good time to trudge to the food market at the Biscuit Mill and return with the ingredients for a delicious meal. Rye breads and cheeses, packets of spices and armloads of exotic flowers. We'll start a slow pot of oxtail in white wine, or pork belly with star anise in cider. While the rain lashes the windows, we'll relax with books in front of the fire and wait for dinner.

Ragout of oxtail

A huge casserole of oxtail is such a satisfying sight after a long day. In this dish I use white wine instead of the usual red, and save the latter for serving with the dish.

- 60 g goose fat
- 1 oxtail, about 1,2 kg, cut up
- 2 large carrots, peeled and chopped
- 1 onion, peeled and chopped; or 4 leeks, sliced and rinsed
- 50 g flour
- 1 bottle dry white wine
- chicken stock to cover
- bouquet garni
- seasoning
- 16 preserved chestnuts (optional)*

Heat the fat in a large casserole, and brown the oxtail pieces. Add the carrots and leeks or onion, brown, and sprinkle with the flour. Stir the mixture and fry it a little more before you add the wine. Empty the bottle of wine into the pot and bring to a fast boil before topping up with the chicken stock. Drop in the bouquet garni.

Simmer gently for about 3 hours – the meat should almost be coming off the bone and the liquid should have reduced to a delicious thick, glossy sauce. Season with salt and pepper.

Remember to remove the bouquet garni before serving the oxtail.

To create a thoroughly French dish, add the chestnuts to the cooked oxtail and warm gently. Serve with couscous and Provençal vegetables.

* These are readily available at good delis.

Moroccan lamb with tomatoes & almonds

This fabulous dish is ideal to share with good friends and honey is the secret.

- olive oil
- 2 kg lamb knuckles
- 2 big onions, quartered
- 2 cinnamon sticks
- 1 t ground ginger
- 1 t saffron
- 6 tomatoes, peeled and chopped
- 2 t ground cinnamon
- 4 T honey
- 2 cloves garlic, chopped
- sea salt and freshly ground black pepper
- slivered almonds to serve

Heat a little olive oil in a deep, heavy-bottomed pot, and brown the knuckles.

Remove and set aside. Add the onions, cinnamon sticks, ginger and saffron to the oil. Toss the onions with the spices until they are slightly cooked. Put the knuckles back into the pot. Drain the chopped tomatoes through a sieve into the pot, and set the pulp aside.

Steam the knuckles in the tomato juice for 2 minutes before adding enough water to cover. Stew the meat over a low heat – you'll need something between 60 and 90 minutes – until tender. Remove the meat and cinnamon sticks; discard the latter.

Add the chopped tomatoes, ground cinnamon, honey and garlic to the sauce in the pot and simmer for 3 minutes. Return the knuckles to the sauce and reheat. Season to taste.

To serve, garnish with a handful of lightly grilled slivered almonds.

The dish is delicious with couscous.

Couscous with fresh parsley

An easy technique to guarantee a heap of lovely, light couscous. Just always remember to get your hands in there. Couscous needs air.

- 500 g couscous
- 5 ml sea salt
- 1 T olive oil
- handful flat-leaf parsley, chopped
- 2 T spring onions, chopped
- 3 T pine nuts, lightly pan-toasted

An easy, fairly foolproof and really therapeutic technique to guarantee a heap of lovely, light couscous is to pour the dry couscous into a glass bowl, season with the salt, and work the olive oil through with a fork. Try to get all the grains oiled.

In the meantime, boil a kettle of water. Pour enough over the couscous to just cover it. I always judge the level by sight … about half a centimetre above the couscous level will do it! Immediately cover the bowl tightly with cling wrap or a plate, and let it stand for 15 minutes.

Remove the cover and gently fork the steaming couscous onto a warm serving dish.

Now for the fun part! Remove your rings and wash your hands. The idea is to 'get air' into the grains. Lift handfuls of couscous as high as possible without making too much of a mess. Gently rub the grains together to break up any clumps. The grains will fall back into the serving dish – feather light.

Once you have worked through all the couscous, gently fold in the parsley, spring onions and pine nuts. And please use your fingers!

I enjoy serving couscous with any really saucy lamb dish.

Venison pot pies

The 'cooking off' of the bones after a hunting trip is always fun. My son used to have shiny cheeks from sucking the marrow from the bones which I scooped out between the rillette in the pot.

- 50 ml olive oil
- 2 kg venison, off the bone (keep the bones)
- 3 pork trotters
- 750 ml dry red wine
- 500 ml chicken stock
- 2 carrots, peeled and sliced in pennies
- 1 celery stick, sliced with leaves
- 4 cloves garlic
- 2 leeks, sliced in pennies and rinsed
- 2 bay leaves
- 8 peppercorns
- 4 juniper berries
- seasoning
- 100 g butter
- 2 rolls puff pastry, thawed
- 1 egg

Heat the olive oil gently in your biggest pot. Fry the venison until it is slightly browned. Add the bones and the trotters. Pour the wine over the meat and bring to the boil. Add the chicken stock. Toss in the carrots, celery, garlic, leeks, bay leaves, peppercorns and juniper berries. Turn the heat down slightly, cover, and simmer for about 3 hours. The meat from the trotters should come off the bone, and the venison should be completely soft. Remove the meat and bones from the pot and reduce any leftover liquid. Let the venison cool slightly and shred it. Debone the trotters and combine the meats in the reduced stock. Season to taste.

Butter 8 clay ramekins and divide the mixture between them. Roll open the thawed puff pastry and cut 4 ramekin-sized rounds out of each sheet. Place the pastry on top and over each ramekin, pinching gently with your fingers around the side of the dish in order to secure the dough. With a sharp knifepoint, make tiny criss-cross cuts into the dough to allow the steam to escape during cooking. Whisk the egg and brush the top of each pie to glaze.

Bake the pies for 25 minutes in an oven preheated to 220 deg C/Gas 7 until the pastry is a shiny, deep golden colour.

Serve immediately with gusto!

Honeyed sweet potatoes

To be enjoyed with galjoen or snoek ... or just about any main dish ... Good enough for the gods!

- 8 sweet potatoes
- 50 g butter
- 50 g castor sugar
- 100 ml honey

Halve each sweet potato and place in an ovenproof dish. Put a thin slice of butter on each half. Sprinkle with the sugar. Add water to the pan just to cover the base. Cover with foil. Steam/bake the sweet potatoes at 180 deg C/Gas 4 for 20 minutes. Remove the foil.

Spoon a dollop of honey over, and return uncovered to the oven for another 15 minutes. (Add a handful of cinnamon sticks to the pan for fabulous flavour.)

The sweet potatoes should be caramelised and totally yummy!

Pork belly with star anise, cider & honey

Serves 6

*Fantastically satisfying to dig into.
I love it!*

- 2 T olive oil
- 4 spring onions, chopped
- 1 fat finger of ginger (or to taste), peeled and chopped
- 1 star anise
- 4 cloves
- 250 ml semi-sweet apple cider
- 125 ml honey
- 2 ℓ chicken stock
- 2 fresh bay leaves
- 6 sage leaves, chopped
- 2 kg pork belly, bones removed, cut into bite-size pieces

Place the olive oil, spring onions, ginger, star anise, cloves, cider, honey and chicken stock into a large pot and bring to a simmering boil. Tip in the herbs and simmer for about 10 minutes. Add the pork, turn the heat down and cover. After about 30 minutes, remove the lid and cook, uncovered, over a really low heat for another couple of hours, keeping an eye on it so it does not cook dry. Add some cider if needed. And have a glass or two yourself.

Once the meat is deliciously soft, spoon it onto a warm serving platter and keep warm.

Scoop most of the fat off the cooking liquid and discard. Reduce the rest of the liquid until it is thick and syrupy.

Spoon the sauce over the meat and serve accompanied by tiny boiled potatoes.

Spaghetti with pine nuts, sage & lemon

Easy, quick and absolutely delicious.

- 750 g spaghetti
- 125 ml olive oil
- 20 sage leaves
- 200 g pine nuts, toasted
- zest and juice of 1 lemon
- 2 cloves garlic, chopped
- salt and freshly ground black pepper

Cook the spaghetti in a large pot of salted boiling water.

Heat the olive oil in a pan and fry the sage leaves in the oil until crisp. Take care not to burn the oil.

Drain the pasta and return to the pot. Add all the ingredients, including the sage leaves and olive oil, season well and serve.

Chapter 7

In the kitchen

The kitchen in St George's Villa is so tiny that the person sitting at the end of the small table has to play the part of food and beverage manager and supply the cook with what she needs from the fridge! There's not too much room for moving about.

In this tiny space we make meals that are served straight from the stove or oven. Easy chicken pie, coq au vin or tomato stew ... comfort food that lures my son and his friends on trains from their university campus to a late-night plate of home cooking and an icy beer. Blissful times.

Chicken & leek pie

This stylish-looking pie works across both family and formal occasions.

- 2 sheets puff pastry, thawed
- 1 free-range chicken
- 12 chicken wings
- 750 ml white wine
- bouquet garni
- 1 carrot, peeled and chopped
- 3 cloves garlic
- seasoning
- 5 T olive oil
- 600 g leeks, washed and sliced into pennies
- 2 T butter
- 2 T plain flour
- 125 ml full cream
- 3 eggs

Line a buttered springform pan with one sheet of puff pastry. Prick a few holes in the pastry with a fork. Keep it in the fridge until you need it.

Heat a large casserole, put the chicken and the wings in the pot, and add the wine.

While it's coming to a gentle boil, add the bouquet garni, carrot, garlic and some seasoning.

Add water to cover and let the chicken simmer until the meat falls off the bones.

Remove from the heat. Spoon the chicken out of the casserole and debone. Pour the fabulous stock through a sieve and keep aside.

In the meantime, pour the olive oil into a heated pan, add the leeks and fry them until they are soft and glossy. Take a medium casserole, melt the butter and stir in the flour with one hand while adding the chicken stock with the other. Fun! Keep adding the stock until you have a thick sauce with a creamy consistency. Remove from the heat. Add the cream. Whisk the eggs and fold them into the sauce. Finally, add the leeks and mix well.

Fold in the chicken, and spoon the whole lot into the prepared pastry shell. Cover with the second sheet of pastry, folding gently around the edges, and trim where necessary.

Bake this delicious pie for 1 hour at 180 deg C/Gas 4. Serve with a green salad.

Coq au vin

Serve in soup plates with lovely crusty bread for mopping up the sauces.

- 500 g bacon, chopped
- olive oil
- 1,2 kg jointed chicken or, if available, 2 poussin, halved
- 2 onions, sliced and chopped
- 2 carrots, peeled and chopped
- 4 cloves garlic, crushed
- 2 huge marrow bones (beef)
- large bouquet garni
- 4 bay leaves
- 1 t thyme
- freshly ground black pepper
- 30 g flour
- 2 bottles red wine
- 1 *l* chicken stock
- 20 small onions
- 500 g mushrooms
- 50 ml butter
- 25 g sugar
- 2 T brandy

Braise the bacon in some olive oil until the fat runs. Remove. Brown the chicken in the same oil. Add the onions, carrots, garlic, marrow bones, bouquet garni and herbs.

Sprinkle with black pepper and flour, and stir these in before adding the wine and stock. Cook at a slow simmer for about 45 minutes until the chicken is tender.

In the meantime, boil the onions until they're just soft.

A few minutes before you're ready to serve, brown the mushrooms in olive oil and add to the casserole. Caramelise the onions in butter and sugar, and add. Flambée the brandy – it's easiest to do this if you warm it in a small pan over a low flame first – and pour it over the chicken. Serve in soup plates with crusty bread on the side.

Spicy shoulder of lamb with aubergine caviar

This is a perfect main course: lamb with a creamy helping of aubergine caviar.

- 1 T sea salt
- 1 T coriander seeds
- 1 T fennel seeds
- 1 t freshly ground black pepper
- 125 ml extra virgin olive oil
- 1 shoulder of lamb
- 500 ml chicken or lamb stock
- 6 cloves garlic, peeled
- 500 ml fresh basil, chopped

Finely grind the salt, coriander seeds, fennel seeds and black pepper using a mortar and pestle. Blend the olive oil into the spicy mix and then rub it into the shoulder of lamb. And please use your fingers!

Bake the shoulder in a covered roasting dish at 180 deg C/Gas 4 for about 2 hours, or until succulently tender. Remove from the pan and keep warm.

Pour the stock into a medium-sized saucepan, add the pan juices and garlic cloves, and bring to a rapid boil. Reduce to a saucy quality. Add the chopped basil and serve immediately with aubergine caviar.*

This is wonderful with a Shiraz …

* Turn the page for this recipe.

Aubergine caviar

Superb with a meat dish, but served with crusty bread it also makes a great snack before dinner.

- 2 medium aubergines, whole
- 2 T olive oil
- 3 cloves garlic, peeled and chopped
- 4 salad onions, finely chopped
- juice of 1 lemon
- 2 T flat-leaf parsley, chopped
- 250 ml crème fraîche
- sea salt and freshly ground black pepper to taste

Prick the aubergines all over with a fork and rub them with olive oil before roasting them at about 200 deg C/Gas 6 for 15 to 20 minutes, until completely tender. Remove from the oven, let them cool a bit ... for obvious reasons! ... then cut in half and scoop the flesh into a mixing bowl. Add the garlic, salad onions, lemon juice, parsley and crème fraîche and gently fold together. Season to taste and serve with the shoulder of lamb.

Tomato & lamb stew ancienne

A little trip down nostalgia lane. We all used to love coming home on a wintry day to the smell of this stew.

- 2 T extra virgin olive oil
- 25 g butter
- 2 kg stewing lamb, preferably including some ribs and flank
- 1 T flour
- 3 red onions, peeled and roughly sliced
- 1 ℓ chicken stock
- 8 small potatoes, peeled
- 8 ripe tomatoes, peeled and sliced
- 5 cloves garlic, chopped
- pinch dried chilli
- 2 t sugar
- sea salt and freshly ground black pepper to taste
- handful young, fresh basil leaves

Heat the olive oil in a large casserole dish. Melt the butter in the warm oil and brown the lamb. Dust with the flour. Add the chopped onions to the pot and fry with the meat for about 5 minutes, and then pour the stock into the casserole. Bring the meat to a slow simmer and allow to cook gently, uncovered, for an hour before adding the potatoes, tomatoes, garlic, chilli and sugar. Simmer for at least another hour over a low heat until the meat falls off the bones. If necessary, add a little more stock or water.

Taste, season and spoon into a serving dish.

Garnish with the basil and serve with a steaming dish of basmati rice.

This will be delicious with a bottle or two of Shiraz.

Pot-au-feu

Serves 8

Another gem from the heart of the French countryside.

Meat

- 1 ox tongue
- 1 kg brisket, off the bone and trimmed of fat
- 2 pork trotters, cleaned
- 5 leeks, sliced into pennies and washed
- 1 head garlic
- bouquet garni
- 20 peppercorns
- 1 t dried fennel seeds
- 750 ml dry white wine
- sea salt

Vegetables

- 16 baby carrots, peeled
- 8 baby leeks, trimmed and washed
- 8 small courgettes, topped and tailed

To cook the meat, place the tongue, brisket and trotters in a large pot with the leeks, garlic, bouquet garni, peppercorns and fennel seeds. Pour in the wine, and add cold water to cover if necessary. Bring to a rapid boil, then turn down to a slow simmer. Keep simmering for about 90 minutes, making sure it never boils and skimming off any scum that rises.

Once the brisket is soft enough to slice, remove it from the pot. Test with a sharp knife whether the meat is tender enough for your taste. Allow the tongue and trotters to continue cooking until really soft. Again you need to test for tenderness with a sharp knife.

When it's ready, remove the meat from the pot and skin the tongue. Return all the meats to the pot to warm through. Season to taste with sea salt.

In the meantime, cook the vegetables separately. The carrots and leeks can be cooked in a saucepan with salted water, while the courgettes are probably better off steamed. Try to time the vegetables to be ready at roughly the same time as the meat. You will need about 10 minutes … and don't overcook the courgettes … you want them slightly crunchy!

To serve, slice the brisket and tongue onto a large serving platter. Serve the trotters whole … fabulous to barter for them! Arrange the vegetables around the meat. This truly authentic dish goes brilliantly with a bowl of aioli and some baby potatoes.

And, of course, a glass or two/three of gutsy Shiraz.

Chicken in the pot

According to legend, Henry IV, king of France (1553-1610), had the dreamed of a kingdom where every man could afford a chicken in the pot on a Sunday.

- 1 free-range chicken
- 1 T olive oil
- 750 ml dry white wine
- 250 ml chicken stock
- 1 bouquet garni
- 2 whole carrots, peeled
- 4 whole courgettes
- 6 baby leeks, washed
- 4 cloves garlic, peeled
- 1 celery stick
- salt and freshly ground black pepper

Place the chicken in a large pot. Pour the olive oil over it … just for a bit of gloss! Add the wine and stock and bring to a gentle simmer. Add the bouquet garni, carrots, courgettes, leeks, garlic and celery.

Keep the pot simmering until the chicken meat is so soft that it is falling off the bones. Season generously.

Using a large ladle, gently lift the chicken out of the pot and arrange all the tender vegetables around it on a warm platter. This is comfort food at its best.

Eat immediately.

Cauliflower roasted in olive oil

Serves 4

A lovely, healthy side dish.

- 1 cauliflower, broken into small florets
- 60 ml olive oil
- 1 T butter, melted
- salt and freshly ground black pepper
- 100 ml almond flakes, lightly browned

Preheat the oven to 180 deg C/Gas 4. Place the cauliflower in a roasting dish and drizzle the olive oil and butter over it. Roast for about 20 minutes before turning the pieces. They should be a lovely golden brown. Roast for another 20 minutes, remove from the oven, season, garnish with the almonds and serve.

Chapter 8

Around the yellowwood table

All older houses have formal dining rooms. Mine is graced by a lovely table found in the Karoo many years ago. It is full of scratches and marks, and during a recent polishing session I found a small signature made by my son when he was little, cleverly hidden away amongst the rest of the hieroglyphics!

On the rare night we have guests around this table, the fare would be elegant ... double-reduced stock or sauce Albufera with chicken, or lamb shanks with pancetta and creamy risotto. We love getting out the tall crystal glasses and large napkins. Silver and bone. Old memories ...

Chicken breasts with sauce Albufera

Serves 8

Sumptuous Albufera sauce is also divine with any game birds.

- 50 ml goose fat or olive oil
- 8 chicken breasts
- sea salt and pepper to taste

Sauce

- 2 ℓ chicken stock
- 12 chicken wings
- 1 celery stick, sliced
- 3 carrots, peeled and sliced
- 1 leek, trimmed and sliced
- 1 bouquet garni
- 2 bay leaves
- 10 peppercorns
- 25 ml full cream
- 100 g foie gras – if you can't find fresh, a 125 g tin will do. Eat what's left over behind the kitchen door – I do it regularly!

Heat the fat or oil in a flat pan. Fry the chicken breasts quickly on both sides and put on a warm platter to rest. Season to taste and serve with the sauce Albufera.

Sauce

Bring the chicken stock to the boil in a big casserole. Add the wings, celery, carrots, leek, bouquet garni, bay leaves and peppercorns, and cook until the meat is almost falling off the bones and all the flavours are fully integrated. If you're tempted to quickly steal and gobble down a wing, do it now … they're delish! Remove the casserole from the heat and pour the contents through a sieve and back into the pot. Let it simmer until the stock has reduced by half.

Add the cream and the foie gras. Stir gently until the foie gras has melted into the sauce and the sauce has thickened. Spoon this sublime sauce over the chicken breasts and serve with crushed potatoes.

Lamb shanks with pancetta, fennel & risotto

If you're in doubt about what to serve, and if you really want to spoil your friends, just DO it!

- 2 T goose fat
- 10 lamb shanks, seasoned with salt and pepper
- 2 medium carrots, peeled and chopped
- 1 celery stick, chopped
- 6 cloves garlic
- 250 g pancetta, cut in cubes
- 1 T fennel seeds
- 1 bottle dry white wine
- bouquet garni
- 1 ℓ lamb stock

Melt the fat in your biggest pot on top of the stove. Brown the shanks. Add the carrot, celery and garlic, and fry quickly. Add the pancetta and fennel seeds. Pour the white wine over the shanks, add the bouquet garni and stock, and simmer gently for about 2 hours, until the shanks are very tender.

Remove the meat from the pot and keep warm. Reduce the remaining stock and season. Serve with a creamy Gorgonzola and truffle oil risotto (see overleaf).

Creamy risotto with Gorgonzola & truffle oil

Ideal for serving with lamb shanks.

- 100 g butter
- 3 leeks, chopped
- 600 g risotto rice
- half bottle dry white wine
- lamb stock from your shank pot (see page 144)
- 250 ml cream
- 100 g Gorgonzola
- seasoning
- truffle oil
- parboiled baby carrots and leeks to garnish

Melt the butter and fry the leeks until soft. Add the risotto and fry quickly until all the grains are covered with butter.

Add the wine, and stir constantly until the alcohol has evaporated and most of the wine has been absorbed. Ladle some stock out of the lamb shank pot – make sure you pick up some of the pancetta at the same time – and stir until it's absorbed.

Stir some more.* Stir. Keep stirring. Add more stock and stir.

More stock and stirring are needed until the risotto is nearly ready – it should be slightly al dente. Add cream. Stir it in, and add the Gorgonzola. Stir some more. Add seasoning. Stir until the risotto is beautifully creamy and tasty.

Dish up in huge soup bowls, add a dash of truffle oil, place a shank on top, and garnish with the parboiled baby carrots and leeks.

* This is absolutely fabulous for upper arms!

Osso bucco

This old recipe from Milan makes a simple and lovely meal that is especially good on a cold night.

- 12 pieces veal shank, 4 cm thick
- plain flour, seasoned
- 60 ml olive oil
- 60 g butter
- garlic to taste
- 250 ml dry white wine
- 1 bay leaf
- pinch allspice
- pinch cinnamon

Gremolata
- 2 lemons
- 1 large bunch fresh parsley
- 10 cloves garlic, peeled

Dust the shanks with seasoned flour. Heat the oil, butter and garlic in a large, heavy saucepan. Add the shanks and cook for about 15 minutes, until well browned. Stand the shanks on their sides in a single layer, pour in the wine and add the bay leaf, allspice and cinnamon. Cover. Cook at a low simmer for 15 minutes, then add 125 ml warm water. Continue cooking, covered, for about an hour until the meat is very tender. Add more water if needed. Transfer the veal to a warm platter and serve with gremolata.

Gremolata
Zest the lemons and finely chop the parsley. Crush and chop the garlic cloves. Toss them together and sprinkle over the osso bucco just before serving.

Raan

This special leg of lamb hails from Hyderabad, the most famous food region in India.

- 1 leg of lamb, trimmed
- 5 T lemon juice, freshly squeezed
- rind of 2 lemons
- 125 g fresh root ginger, peeled and chopped
- 10 large cloves garlic, peeled and chopped
- 1 t turmeric
- 2 t cumin
- 6 cardamon pods, seeded
- 2 t dried chilli
- ½ t cinnamon
- 3 t sea salt
- 3 bay leaves
- 2 star anise
- 250 g powdered almonds
- 4 T brown sugar
- 500 ml thick, full-cream yoghurt
- ½ t saffron strands, soaked in 2 T boiling water

Use a small sharp knife to make several deep gashes in the leg of lamb.

Use a mortar and pestle to blend the lemon juice, rind, ginger, garlic, turmeric, cumin, cardamon, chilli, cinnamon and salt thoroughly until a thick purée forms. Take a spatula and spread the purée thickly over the entire leg of lamb. Stick the bay leaves and star anise to the meat. Place the covered meat in the fridge for about an hour.

Put the almonds, sugar and half of the yoghurt into an electric blender and purée at high speed. Scrape the almond paste into a mixing bowl and fold the remaining yoghurt into the paste. Remove the lamb from the fridge and spoon the almond paste over the spicy coating.

Cover the lamb and return to the fridge for another 48 hours.

Remove the lamb from the fridge about 2 hours before cooking time to allow the meat to reach room temperature before going into the oven. Heat the oven to 220 deg C/Gas 7 and roast the leg of lamb for 20 minutes. Turn the temperature down to 180 deg C/Gas 4 and cover the meat before returning it to the oven for another 3 hours. Once the meat is cooked and tender, remove it from the oven pan and place it on a serving platter. Remove all excess fat from the pan before pouring the juices into a cooking pot. Add the saffron to the stock and bring to a rapid boil, until the meat juices reduce to become a lovely sauce. Slice the lamb, spoon the sauce over it, and serve with couscous.

Poached salmon with soubise

Soubise is an onion purée which is often added to velvety sauces ... lovely with fish.

- 2 large onions, peeled and thinly sliced
- 175 g butter
- sea salt and freshly ground black pepper
- 1 T extra virgin olive oil
- 1 leek, sliced into pennies and washed
- 1 fennel bulb, trimmed, sliced and washed
- 1 clove garlic
- few sprigs thyme
- 2 bay leaves
- 2 fish heads
- 1 ℓ water
- 125 ml white wine
- 2 T flour
- pinch saffron threads
- 125 ml full cream
- 6 portions salmon or firm-fleshed fish

To prepare the soubise, place the onions in a saucepan with plenty of salted water and bring to the boil. Drain and add 125 g of the butter, salt and pepper. Cover and cook over a gentle heat for about 20 minutes.

In the meantime, prepare the stock. Heat the olive oil in a heavy-based cooking pan and fry the leek, fennel and garlic until softened. Add the thyme, bay leaves, fish heads, water and wine, bring to a simmer and cook for 20 minutes.

Drain the stock through a fine sieve or cloth and pour into a jug.

In a deep cooking pot, melt the rest of the butter and make a roux by adding the flour. Stirring constantly over a medium heat, add three-quarters of the fish stock until you have a thick velouté.

Fold the soubise into the velouté, add the saffron and cream, and allow the sauce to cook gently for a minute or two. Taste and season.

To cook the fish, pour the rest of the stock into a large pan and bring to the boil. Turn down the heat slightly. Slide the fish portions into the simmering stock and poach for about 6 minutes, taking care not to overcook the fish.

Serve in large soup plates. Place a portion of fish in the middle of each plate and spoon the delicious sauce over it. Garnish with a sprig of thyme and serve with tiny new potatoes and a glass of rosé.

Chicken with lemongrass & ginger

Quick, easy and lovely!

- soft part of 5 stems lemongrass, chopped
- 1 fat finger ginger, grated
- 3 cloves garlic, crushed
- 2 red chillies, chopped
- 500 g chicken thighs, skinned, deboned and cut in bite-sized bits
- 75 ml olive oil
- salt and freshly ground black pepper
- 1 brown onion, chopped
- 4 spring onions, chopped
- 1 t soy sauce
- 1 t brown sugar

In a mortar, pound the lemongrass, ginger, garlic and chilli to a paste. Toss the chicken with some of the olive oil and the paste until it is well covered. Season lightly.

Heat the rest of the oil in a wok. Add the chicken and stir-fry for 5 minutes before adding the chopped onion, spring onions, soy sauce and sugar. Continue cooking until the sugar has dissolved. Serve immediately with lightly steamed rice.

Index

Spicy shoulder of lamb with aubergine
   caviar 128
Stuffed lamb shoulder 62
Tomato & lamb stew ancienne 132
Tripe & trotters with white wine 84

Pasta
Spaghetti with pine nuts, sage & lemon 120

Pork
Cassoulet 90
Pork belly with star anise, cider & honey 118

Side dishes
Aubergine caviar 130
Carrots with roasted walnuts in orange juice 74
Cauliflower roasted in olive oil 138
Couscous with fresh parsley 112
Creamy risotto with Gorgonzola & truffle oil 146
Honeyed sweet potatoes 116
Potatoes with rosemary 16
Puy lentils with prosciutto 36
Sweet potatoes with ginger & chillies 28
Vegetables with persillade 88

Venison
Rabbit in red wine with chestnuts 86
Venison fillet pan-fried with ginger & sage 26
Venison in red wine & chocolate sauce 98
Venison pot pies 114

Glossary

aioli: garlic mayonnaise

al dente: still slightly chewy; not too soft

Albufera: so named after an original dedication to Antonin Careme to Marshall Suchet, Duc d'Albufera; most commonly chicken and duck dishes

ancienne: ancient

au gratin: baked or browned with breadcrumbs

beurre noisette: butter that has been gently heated in a frying pan until it is a dark golden colour and gives off a nutty smell

blanch: to bring water to a boil, add ingredients and boil for no more than 2 minutes

bouquet garni: selection of aromatic herbs and plants, tied together in a small bundle and used to add flavour to sauces and stocks

braise: to lightly brown in fat and then cook slowly with a lid in a small amount of liquid

canard: duck

caramelise: to convert to a caramel-like consistency

cassoulet: stew

chèvre: cheese made from goat's milk

chiffonade: very fine julienne of vegetables, usually associated with leafy herbs, lettuces or greens

cognac: world-famous brandy distilled from wine, made in the region of Cognac in France

confit: piece of meat cooked in its own fat and stored; covered in its own fat to preserve it

coq au vin: chicken with bacon, onions, mushrooms, wine and flambéed brandy

couscous: traditional North African dish made with semolina

crème fraîche: cream to which a lactic acid has been added which thickens the cream and gives it a distinctive sharp flavour without souring the cream

deglaze: adding a drop of wine to a used pan and scraping all the bits and pieces full of flavour together before producing a magnificent sauce

dollop: scoop

emulsify: to combine two or more liquids (e.g. eggs, oil and lemon juice) in such a way that they are equally dispersed and produce an emulsion (e.g. mayonnaise)

entrecôte: rib steak

flambée: to flame with cognac or other alcohol

foie gras: goose or duck liver that is enlarged by methodically fattening the bird

glaze: to cover with a shiny coating

gremolata: mixture of chopped parsley, garlic and lemon peel

julienne: cut into thin sticks

jus de cuisson: natural juices or gravy

pancetta: cured, unsmoked pork belly that is rolled and tied

parboil: to boil until partially cooked

persillade: mixture of chopped parsley and garlic

pistou: pesto

pouch: to lightly boil in wine or water

polenta: cornmeal porridge that is the traditional basic dish of northern Italy

pot-au-feu: essentially French dish which provides at the same time soup, boiled meat and vegetables

prosciutto: Italian word for ham, usually referring to the raw hams of Parma in Italy

purée: creaming cooked foods through a sieve or with a food processor

ragout: stew made from meat, poultry, game, fish or vegetables that is cooked in a thickened liquid and flavoured with herbs and seasonings

reduce: to concentrate or thicken a sauce or soup by boiling

risotto: creamy Italian rice dish

roux: equal amounts of butter and flour used to make or thicken sauces

roux brun: same as a roux but cooked longer until it has browned slightly

saffron: spice derived from the dried stigma of the saffron crocus; has a pungent smell and bitter flavour

saucisses de Toulouse: sausages from Toulouse

saucisson à cuire: cooked sausage

saucisson: sausage

sauté: to cook meat, fish or vegetables in fat until brown

sear: to scorch or burn the surface

soubise: purée of onions mixed into a thick white sauce

stock: flavoured liquid base for making a sauce, stew or braised dish

strain: to filter through either a strainer, colander or cloth

sweat: to cook vegetables in fat over a gentle heat so that they become soft and their juices are concentrated in the cooking fat

tagliolini: flat ribbon pasta, narrower than tagliatelle

tapenade: paste made of cured black olives, seasoned with olive oil, garlic, anchovies, capers and lemon

truss: to tie

velouté: basic sauce made with chicken or veal stock and thickened with a roux

zest: coloured or outer rind of any citrus fruit